10

COMMANDMENTS OF THE WORKING
WIFE

10
COMMANDMENTS OF THE WORKING
WIFE

Dr. Ankrehah Trimble Johnson, DO

10 COMMANDMENTS OF THE WORKING WIFE

Published by Purposely Created Publishing Group™

Copyright © 2018 Ankrehah Johnson

All rights reserved.

No part of this book may be reproduced, distributed or transmitted in any form by any means, graphic, electronic, or mechanical, including photocopy, recording, taping, or by any information storage or retrieval system, without permission in writing from the publisher, except in the case of reprints in the context of reviews, quotes, or references.

Limit of Liability / Disclaimer of Warranty: While the publisher and author have used their best efforts in preparing this book, they make no representations or warranties with the respect to the accuracy or completeness of the contents of this book and specifically disclaim any implied warranties of fitness for a particular purpose. No warranty may be created or extended by sales representatives or written sales materials. The advice and strategies contained herein may not be suitable for your situation. You should consult with a doctor where appropriate. Neither the publisher nor author shall be liable for any loss or damages including but not limited to special, incidental, consequential or other damages.

Printed in the United States of America

ISBN: 978-1-948400-18-3

Special discounts are available on bulk quantity purchases by book clubs, associations and special interest groups. For details email: sales@publishyourgift.com or call (888) 949-6228.

For information logon to: www.PublishYourGift.com

Dedication

This book is dedicated to:

My husband, Jay, for allowing me to be an amazing working wife and always keeping me on my toes.

Our Zoe Grace for adding the title of Mommy to my working wife resume: you give us life every day!

The working wives in my life who do it effortlessly every day, and who I try and make proud just by grinding as hard as I can.

My mom, Dr. Cathy Trimble, who I watched get her own doctorate while she balanced family with work and also cared for her own mother towards the end of her life.

My sister, Angelica Trimble Luma: we were married two weeks apart and have enjoyed the ups and downs of marriage together.

My mother-in-love, Gwen Coley, who does not play! You've taught me the art of being a mama bear and not worrying about what others think!

The ladies of Wife Matters with Doctor Kre: you motivate me to motivate others.

This book is also in the memory of one of my best friends, my Spelman sister, my line sister, a woman who was a boss of a working wife: Dr. Latonya Hendricks Carter. I know you are proud and would have a ton of commentary. Fly high in heaven, phenomONE!

Finally, this book is for you, my fabulous working wife who has invested so much in others that you might've forgotten about yourself. But you've invested in yourself for a change by reaching for this book—you won't regret it! #wifewin #fullplate #wifedown #allworkingwivesmatter

Table of Contents

Introduction 1

Chapter 1: All Working Wives Matter 5

Chapter 2: Mommy, May I? 9

Chapter 3: Being His Wife: He Put a Ring on It 13

Chapter 4: Self-Care: Is It worth It? 17

Chapter 5: Daily Affirmations: Do You
Need Them? 21

Chapter 6: Are You Lifting Him Up? 25

Chapter 7: Do You Take Care of You? 29

Chapter 8: Mommy, You Are the Best! 33

Chapter 9: With All This Work, Where
Does Sex Fit In? 37

Chapter 10: Competition Has Its Place 41

Chapter 11: Goal Digging 45

Chapter 12: Art of Delegation 49

Chapter 13: Raising a Brilliant Kid 53

Bonus: Ten Commandments of the Working Wife 47

Thank You 59

About Doctor Kre 61

Introduction

Dear Working Wife,

Wouldn't it be great to wake up to a nanny who's already gotten the kids ready for the day? A housekeeper who's cleaned the house? Grounds-keepers to man the yard? A driver to drop the kids off each day and to take you wherever you please? An assistant to gather the groceries and be at your beck and call? All the people and resources that will leave you well rested, always in a great mood, and early for work, for church, and for other activities?

If you are a working wife, I'm sure you are or you've been the one person who wears a lot of these hats. You know what it's like to have very little time to survive, let alone time for you to be rested, chipper, and spry. Trust me, you are *not* alone.

This feeling of being overwhelmed lies deeply in the hearts of many working wives, and we so often act like the balancing act is not an issue that we actually end up making ourselves sick. More often than physically, we are mentally sick; and when we are mentally sick, our bodies begin to display physical manifestations of illness. We suffer headaches and changes in bowel habits. We over-eat, gain weight, and get pain in our joints. All of this leads us into further states of unhappiness.

This, my dear, is the superwoman complex at its finest. Often times, you don't realize you have it until you have it and your coworkers, your husband, or even your kids pull you aside and say, "Honey, something just isn't right with you." This can definitely be a blow to our egos because, as superwomen, there should not be anything (outwardly) wrong with us because we handle everything—and *I mean everything*!

The rules of a working wife are here to tell you that, first off, you are bad to the bone and a force to be reckoned with. But even forces need assistance and self-reflection every now and then. Take this opportunity to think about someone who you have not thought of in quite a while: you, girlfriend!

So, grab a grown-up beverage and some highlighters, and enjoy this journey of falling in love with your charms and your flaws all over again. You won't regret it!

Doctor Kre
Chief Wifeologist

All Working Wives Matter

Any working wife usually hustles full-time by day for a check (that is considerably less than what her male counterparts earn) and full-time by night for sheer appreciation. Most working wives, by nature, are driven by some goal; many times, their work goals trickle down and interfere with their life goals. More importantly, life begins to interfere with their work goals.

In order to be the best career-oriented wife, we must learn to say words like: No! Not now! It can wait! Stop! For most of us, any of those phrases instantly gives us hives and nervous stomachaches because, given the proactive way that we are wired, we aren't "done" physically or mentally until every item on the to-do list is checked off and perfectly completed.

In order to maximize your time during the workday and minimize the guilt in the back of your mind, you must set a "stop time." This is the non-negotiable deadline at some point in your night at which you stop your busying around, regardless of whether every item on your to-do list is done or not. Here is the beauty of having a stop time: you will begin to organize your time more carefully and get more done, but you will no longer feel guilty if every single bullet on your to-do list is not perfectly executed. You will proudly say that you did everything you could today and there is always tomorrow to do more. Then go right on off to sleep!

This is the kind of advice and encouragement that I want to offer in this book. All working wives matter so much to me because, for the past five years, I too have been a dedicated member of the working wives club. I am a board-certified family medicine physician and I have a solo general medical practice outside of Birmingham, Alabama. Due to my demanding line of work, I know the importance of having to make changes to my day at the last minute to accommodate my own sick child while I also care for everyone else. I know the hurt of having to miss school plays because I wasn't informed far enough in advance to clear my schedule. I know the hassle of having to hire someone to pick up my baby from day care while my husband and I both work late since we're both entrepreneurs. I know the pressure of feeling like I have to make a choice between being a businesswoman and homemaker. I've been through it all!

So, working wife, I want you to know that we've all had these thoughts, whether we've said them out loud or not. You are not in this alone. You really do matter!

Think About It

[1] What will be your stop time? What are some things that you can change in your daily routine so that you have more free time at night? (i.e. get to work earlier, work through part of your lunch, etc.)

[2] How many nights a week do you usually work late? How can you adjust your schedule and cut that down to two late nights a week or less?

[3] Based on your level of education and time on this job, have you ever had a raise? Is your salary competitive? What are the men in your same position earning? What can you do to be more competitive?

Mommy, May I?

If there was a parenting manual that came with each baby you birthed, then life would be much simpler. But when did working wives ever take the easy way out? We love a good challenge. However, we eventually get to a point of asking: where's the balancing point for parenting to intersect with career? Well, there isn't one, *unless* we make one for ourselves. We must choose to be intentional about "mommy-ing."

First, let your kids know that they are a priority in your everyday routine. Many working wives are unable to make school plays, donuts with other moms, mid-day teacher conferences, or even holiday lunches. Despite what others may say, you are a working wife and mom: do *not* feel guilty because you have mandatory work events that take your time away from certain activities with and/or for your kids. Instead, focus on the days that you do have available and try to make it to major moments that embody your kids' special milestones. In this day and age, technology makes it so that, even if you are away, you don't have to feel like you are away. There are countless video chat apps that make this separation a little easier, so stay connected with your kids and avoid the guilt.

You can easily make up for missed time by scheduling Mommy and Me time with each of your kids every week, during which they have your undivided attention. No TV. No cellphones. No emails. Just a good movie or cartoon or whatever they choose—make these times a part of your weekly routine and stick to it. These bonding moments are what you want to have etched in both of your minds in the years to come. Your child may not remember that you were employee of the month five times over, but they will remember the memories you made together during one very special Mommy and Me time. They will remember learning to cook with you. They will remember watching the same show week in and week out with you, and will probably still watch it long after they are grown-ups. Make the time you have count!

Think About It

[1] Do you have a set Mommy and Me time for your kids (despite their ages)? If not, decide on a date and time then put it on your calendar as a reoccurring event.

[2] Do you know what types of activities/hobbies interest your kids? List them and see how you can include them in Mommy and Me time.

[3] Do you know what's relevant in pop culture and the latest social media trends? Know what's going on in your kids' world so that you can educate them appropriately (better you than their friends, right?). What will you do when you need to explain to your kids that you don't want them looking at or following a particular trend?

Being His Wife: He Put a Ring on It

In a perfect world, you'd work half days so that you can come home and cook a fresh meal for your family. You'd freshen up afterwards so you can greet you husband with a kiss and a cocktail when he arrives home. You'd have the kids fed, bathed, and in bed by 8 P.M. so that, for the rest of the night, you can talk about your day and his day. Then you'd serve him dessert: you.

However, for busy working wives, this is nothing but a dream at best. If your life is anything like mine, you work until 5:25 P.M., rush to get the kid from daycare at 5:55 P.M. (daycare closes at 6 P.M.), run home, and warm up something fast like hotdogs, grilled cheese, or even cereal, all while your kid yells because she didn't take a nap at daycare. You are too worn out to really hear how his day went because your day was so crappy and it isn't over yet. You have another hour or two of work to complete so that you can meet that impending deadline. You have every intention of having "grown-up" time after the kid goes to bed, but by the time you are done with your work and showered, he's knocked out in bed. You might fool yourself into thinking you can make up for it in the morning, only to oversleep or have the kid wake up early, knocking at the door to sleep with mommy and dad. Or sometimes, you have to wake up a few hours sooner than planned to complete a whole section of an important project. I'm sure my house isn't the only one that sees this sequence of events more times than not.

I know it's hard with all the time and energy constraints, but you must make a conscious effort to make your husband your #1 priority, stick with it, and mean it. As we climb the ladder of success, some things are left behind and, at times, it's him. He should be able to survive; after all, he is grown, right? Because if it's not work that stressing you, it's the kids, their homework, their hobbies, and after-school activities. Before you know it, your only common goal with your husband are the kids and bills. Where did the time go? Where did the love go? Where did the regular sex go? The intimacy? The long talks? Alone time? All of it is buried under your work and his work. And if you both aren't careful, you'll drift apart in pursuit of the next promotion or being super parents. Don't forget that you both have needs and you both need one another.

So, what's the solution? Wifey-in' ain't easy! The answer lies in your priorities. Your job will require as much of you as you are willing to give. It's up to you to draw the line in the sand, mentally. You must set attainable goals in order to have more time for your husband. That may mean hiring help to pick up the kids from school so you can have some alone time with your man before it's too late and you are too tired. It may mean deciding, "I will only work late once or twice this week," and asking him to do the same. It may mean you bring work home but say, "Babe, lets both promise to be done by X time so we can have all of each other's attention." You might want to try waking up a little earlier or getting your kids in bed earlier, perhaps with a monitor. It's all about being creative: perhaps lunch dates for a bite to eat and a quickie?

Only you can decide when enough is enough. You don't want to open your eyes twenty years from now, kids in college, you and your husband at the top of your work game, and realize that you have no idea who you've been sleeping next to. Don't waste so much time on things that don't add direct value to your relationship. Instead, commit to being intentional about making him feel assured that he comes first to you, outside of God and definitely before your job.

Think About It

[1] Do you have a set date night? If not, add at least two days a month to both your calendars, schedule sitters if needed, and make it non-negotiable.

[2] What are some creative ways to spend more one-on-one time with your spouse?

Self-Care: Is It Worth It?

The average over-worked working wife wouldn't trade her busy life for the world: she finds absolute joy in marking off the long to-do list and seeing her family's smiling faces. Still, even superwoman needs time to rest and rejuvenate.

So, what's the recipe for adding time into the day that's just for you, without feeling guilty? It's simple. Decide to make this a choice and add it to your calendar. Decide that this time is non-negotiable for you and just take it. Once it becomes a part of your weekly or monthly routine, then missing it will feel foreign and you'll begin to wonder how you ever went through life without forcing yourself to take care of your needs as much as you care for others.

I hear your thoughts: "Between meetings, school, kids' pick-up, extracurriculars, dinner, and bed, where do I have a second more to add for others, let alone me-time?" Think of it like this: you usually plan your time around everyone else's events, so is it too much to ask of those same people to give you a bit of time to yourself? If you truly feel guilty, I encourage you to talk to your family about creating your routine self-care time. During this family meeting, make it clear to everyone that your adjusting the schedule will not mean slacking or cutting down on the usual family activities. You're just reminding them that you too need and deserve a break. Once this "me-time" is on everyone's agenda, taking care of you becomes mandatory.

Keep these tips in mind to take full advantage of this time:

1. Take a long lunch to get your eyebrows waxed or to get a massage.

2. Find services that will come to you. You can use apps to find any professional you could think of for any and everything. This is how I found my mobile makeup artist!

3. Set reoccurring appointments before you leave the current appointment. That way, once again, it's on your schedule.

4. Set a budget for your me-time.

5. Promise yourself that you will never feel bad about taking time for yourself (you may have to do this often).

6. Make sure to set aside fun me-times and necessary me-times (we'll discuss this a bit later, but I'm talking about doctor's appointments).

7. Have fun doing something you truly enjoy. No pressure, no "I should be doing..."

8. If you have been neglecting your girlfriends, include them in your time, even if it's a quarterly occasion. Get some face-to-face time in.

9. Take pictures of yourself. Watch how you can look and feel younger and happier just by thinking more about yourself.

Think About It

[1] What are some self-care activities you need to do twice a month (at least)?

[2] How much will you budget for your me-time?

[3] List exactly when you will do those activities and which girlfriends you will invite.

Daily Affirmations: Do You Need Them?

Webster defines affirmation as "emotional support or encouragement." You are beautiful. You are loved. You are needed. You are enough. You are blessed. You should be saying every single one of these statements to yourself on a daily basis. Many of us don't affirm ourselves enough and we definitely don't affirm one another enough. We replay all the bad things we are told about ourselves: you are too fat. You are too needy. You aren't pretty enough. You are a burden. You aren't smart enough. Instead of highlighting the beautiful, we underscore the miserable.

Too often, we think of our childhood and the feelings felt when others said things like, "You're so tall," "Your teeth are too big," "You look funny and awkward," and so on. Like it or not, those comments follow us into adulthood. We must break those holds. We must decide that we will no longer allow them to dictate our future because we are bigger than what others think of us. We have grown or will grow to embrace all our little idiosyncrasies, and if we still don't like them, we're grown enough to take care of them! For big glasses, there are contacts. For big teeth, there are braces. For acne, there are dermatologists. Find out what it takes to overcome that "thing," add it into your budget, and gradually overcome! Do it, not to please others, but to find your truth and to set yourself free. Figure out what bothers you the most, find out if it's something you can or want to get fixed, and then get to accepting yourself for who you are!

Repeat after me: "I am enough. I am great, just the way I am. I have so much to offer the world, so my gifts will make room for me." All of you, no matter where you are or what you are doing, must affirm this over and over again, every single day. When you feel down and under-valued, be secure in your validations.

Think About It

[1] Do you have a daily affirmation? If not, list five you can say every day. You may include some of these examples:
   a. I have more than enough each day for me.
   b. I will take the best care of me that I can.
   c. I am an amazing wife.

[2] Encourage your kids to begin speaking their own positive affirmations. What are some that will help your kids think of their own? If they can talk, they are not too young to start.

Are You Lifting Him Up?

There are several Bible passages that say, life and death lie in the power of the tongue. This is especially true in close relationships, such as the one you have with your husband. So much of his motivation, encouragement, and even downfall starts in your mouth.

Do you know your husbands love language? A love language is *how* you or your partner receives love. Often times, you give love in ways that *you* like to receive love, but this may not be how *your partner* wants or needs to receive love. So, knowing your mate's love language helps them feel love in ways that are necessary and real to them. My husband's love language is speaking and being spoken words of affirmation. I know that he feels loved and supported when I say things like, "I am so proud of you for working with five new clients this week for your business" or "I really appreciate you helping with our daughter today."

Some will say, "Well, it's his kid, too. You shouldn't have to say thank you." This is absolutely true, but saying thanks about anything sets a great tone in your home. I know that he flourishes even more when I say how much I appreciate his actions and thought; after all, a little flattery never hurt anyone. That's why, every single day, I find something to say to show him my appreciation and love. Not because his ego needs it, but because it's the way he feels loved. Every single day, I want him to feel most loved by God first, then by me. I am his #1 fan and I take that job so seriously. Plus, the old women used to say, "If you won't make him feel good, someone else will." *And ain't nobody got time for that!* So, I choose to affirm him every day.

When you begin to feel disconnected from your husband, first check your speech and tone. It may not be what you say, but how you say it: a gentle voice can usually turn away wrath and bring in productive conversations. Yes, wifeys, we have our work cut out for us, but do not let a bad day at work cause you to say bad things to your mate. Don't let his secretary or coworker speak kinder words to him than you do. Remember, you are the one he wants as the CEO of his fan club. As far as you should be concerned, that's a one-member club—others need not apply! He wants and needs you to cheer him on. So, let's begin treating him as well as we do our customers, our patients, our bosses, our clients, and our kids. Because he really deserves it.

Think About It

[1] Have you been lifting your husband up or tearing him down? Why?

[2] What are some ways he can feel your love without being touched physically?

Do You Take Good Care of You?

Earlier in the book, we talked about the importance of taking time for yourself to relax, enjoy, and self-love. But I have another question for you: how well do you take care of your physical health? Do you see a general practitioner (not just your OBGYN) on a yearly basis? I bet if you pulled out your calendar right now, you'd see color-coded appointments for everyone: the kids, your clients, your coworkers, your husband. But what color is assigned for you?

Many businesses today mandate their employees to have physical examinations done each year or their premium increases by $200-$500. This new rule forces everyone to stop and get to the doctor. Women in business are one of the most stressed populations and are most likely to die of heart disease. By the time I see some of these women in my office, it's usually because their manager insists that they see someone: the anxiety and stress are written all over their faces and they show up negatively in their overall work performance. I've made the diagnosis of the superwoman complex time after time.

I usually prescribe a superwoman two weeks off work to de-stress, and if she's not better and well rested by the time of her follow-up appointment, I take her off work for even longer. While this may seem harsh, she must be forced to rest because stress can often lead to serious conditions such as high blood pressure, overeating and weight gain, diabetes, anxiety, and depression. I've never had a working wife with this diagnosis who hasn't tearfully agreed with me and reluctantly agreed to the terms of my prescription: resting, relaxing, and rebooting.

Based on evidence-based practices, here are some screenings you must keep in mind:

- 40 years and older: yearly mammograms. If you have a family history of breast cancer, you will need screenings even sooner. Contact your doctor for further details.

- 50 years and older: colonoscopies. If you have a family history of gastrointestinal cancers, you will need screenings even sooner.

- Yearly:
    - Eye exams.
    - Physicals to check cholesterol and blood sugar.
    - Flu shot.
    - Every ten years: Tetanus shot boosters.

Think About It

[1] Have you had your wellness visit this year? If not, schedule one today. If you do not yet have a primary physician, make a list of top doctors in your area. Ask for references if you need them.

[2] Do you know your family history? If not, ask around and get it recorded so you know if you need earlier screenings.

Mommy, You Are the Best!

Music to my ears! You make a good peanut butter and jelly sandwich: "Mommy, you are the best." You buy your kid a toy to reward them for a job well done at school: "Mommy, you are the best." You pick them up from school earlier than your usual: "Mommy, you are the best." Those five words never get old, can never be said too often, and can never be replayed enough. But in order to hear those acclaimed words even once, we must be around. We must be active participants in the rearing of our kids.

Because I work eleven-hour days and my husband's workday doesn't end until at least eight at night, we usually need help. We need someone to pick our daughter up from school, get her dinner three nights a week, bathe her, and we are only home in time for her bedtime routine, if we don't miss it entirely. This means our part-time nanny must be around for at least three times a week. We can only get away with this for now because our daughter is a toddler, but soon, we'll have to figure something else out. Time awaits for no one.

We must decide to what we will give 100%. The honest truth is that there is only one of you and, at different seasons in life, some things will lack percentage-wise. In summers, for instance, I don't work as late because my daughter has a different schedule and I am needed more at home. When I first began this routine, I felt off-track since I wasn't working as many hours. Still, I adjusted fast. I gave quality instead of quantity at work, so I could get in quality and quantity at home! Let's be clear once more: we can't give 100% everywhere all the time! Does that mean you're a failure? No! It means you're realistic.

Build in safe guards and support members who will allow you to keep your stress to a minimum. On my daughter's approved check-out list for daycare, I have family members, close friends, and my amazing receptionist. If something happens, I can ask one of them to run and get her. I don't have to cancel my day or figure out how to be in two places at one time. And I don't feel guilty about it!

In addition, don't forget to set up a system of checks and balances with your spouse. For instance, if it's my late night, my husband orders food so I don't have to think about what to cook or prepare. These are safe systems we have in place so that my worry meter stays as low as possible. My guilt-o-meter doesn't even exist because I've set up systems to make things go as smooth as possible, and because I've promised both myself and my husband that I won't compare my role and my time to those of other mommies.

With all this in place, at the end of very hectic day, my daughter still screams, "Mommy, you are the best!" That is reward enough.

Think About It

[1] What safeguards do you have in place for your kids when you are unavailable?

[2] Do you have hired help? Consider getting help from a nanny, babysitter, or monthly housekeeper. Make a list of jobs that you need help getting done or you just want done to make your life a little easier.

With All This Work, Where Does Sex Fit In?

Think back to early in your marriage when it didn't matter how late you worked or how hard your day was, you still had the desire to be with your husband. You'd do work, do dinner, and then "do" him. But now that years have passed, job demands have increased for you both. You have two kids and a dog, and you wonder how you ever had time to "practice" and work on having another baby. Your plate is full and all the dreams of sex two to three times a week are now just that: dreams.

So, let's talk about sex. First off, never compare the amount of sex you have in a week with how much other married couples have. Say that out loud: your normal is not anyone else's normal. Let's just say that couples between the ages of thirty and forty-five statistically have sex one to two times a week. Remember that life happens: if you are more overwhelmed at work, then sex may happen a little less.

Reversely, if you are more successful at work, climbing the ladder and meeting deadlines, your energy all around might be heightened and you may enjoy more sex. Then, there's sympathy sex: you may use intimacy as a means of feeling closer to your partner when things are rough and even downright bad. As you can see, there are extremes.

So, if you aren't getting down as much as another couple, well frankly, that's none of anyone's business or concern! The only audience you must be trying to please is your husband, an audience of one, so let's throw the rest out the window.

On the flip side, be sure that you aren't so absorbed in yourself and work that weeks go by without any sex. Sex should definitely be a priority to the working wife. It's a way of connecting to your husband and hitting the reset button to de-stress. Sex releases happy hormones and endorphins so your outlook is better, you feel better, and you act better. Trust me, your staff will be very happy if you get some action regularly.

Now, with that being said, not every woman has experienced an orgasm before (this is much more common than you think so don't give any woman a hard time about it). But since we are all goal-oriented, add "orgasm" to you bucket list if you have not yet achieved one. Sex will consistently reunite you with him and you will not regret the bonding experience.

If spontaneity is not always an option, consider adding sex time to your schedule. You can say, "If it has not happened on its own by 'x' day, I will initiate on Friday." Be intentional if nothing else. Often times, women feel that we shouldn't be the initiators of sex. But you're a wife: let that be a myth and keep on with it. Neither you nor your husband will regret it and you will both enjoy the experience.

Think About It

[1] Are you still sexually spontaneous? If not, that's okay! Grab the calendar and add sex to the schedule, if necessary.

[2] Are you open to trying new things sexually with your partner? If so, list what you have always wanted to try.

Competition Has Its Place

Do you remember the adrenaline rush you got when you met your first work deadline? The high you felt when you were recognized as employee of the month? Perhaps you are on track to become partner and it's only been five years. You rock in a male-dominated workplace!

You don't make friends with coworkers because you just...don't. Are you known amongst your peers as being cut throat? Are they "afraid" of you because you are the no-nonsense, sell-them-straight kind of woman? But what about your friend game? When was the last time you had a friendly phone call with your sorority sister, college roommate, or church member? Do you still have these special connections? Have you burned all the bridges because you talk about everyone to everyone? Have you lost your tribe because you give off the vibe that everyone is beneath you because you have "arrived?"

Know that the same competitive drive that propelled you to the top of your game will sometimes drive away your friends. Even the most successful working wife wants a place to be herself and not just her title, somewhere she's "just Susie" and not "Dr. Susie" or "Top 40 Under 40 Susie." Just that homegirl who has a safe place to talk about her insecurities, to laugh about the trashy reality TV she secretly likes, and to brag about all her husband has "taught" her since the last time she had a girl's trip. The working wife yearns to let her hair down because she only allows a few people to see her without the makeup and lashes, without heels, without the weave, not snatched. She's a wife first, a mom second, a friend third, and then whatever her job title after. She shouldn't be ashamed of this order and neither should you.

So, look deep within and around: if your friend circle keeps getting smaller and smaller as you get higher and higher, step back and check yourself. Ask yourself a few questions:

1. Do I always judge others?

2. Am I always eager to find fault in the next wife/woman?

3. Am I always comparing where I am to where she is?

4. Am I full of advice for my friends even when I've never experienced the situation that they are in?

If you answered "yes" to any of these, the issue might be you. So, what can you do to not get bit by the "I'm better than y'all" bug? First, let people progress at their own pace. Leave your judgment stick at home and appreciate differences in all women, even if you disagree with them. They have free will and choice, just like you do. Second, offer advice only when asked and listen to what others have to say. You don't always know everything, but acting like you do can easily hurt or isolate others. Seek out what your friend needs from you and, if she asks, provide.

Keep in mind that you may need to follow-up these steps by offering apologies to any girlfriends you may have offended. Remember, once you apologize it's up to the friends to accept it and you or not—don't get defensive and don't coerce or mock your friends into staying.

Leave high-level competition at work. No one said healthy competition isn't good amongst friends, but only if everyone agrees to it. If not, be available and supportive all the time and, if asked, bow out gracefully when needed.

Think About It

---

[1] Have you ever been labeled as the "too much" friend? The competitive one for no reason?

[2] List the names of girlfriends you may have hurt and with whom you need to set the record right. If you don't remember why you fell apart, now is a good time to check on them and ask.

Goal Digging

Do you remember what you wanted to be when you grew up? Didn't you change your mind a million times? Maybe you changed your major after freshman year in college because that first subject was *not* it. Then you found your passion, your drive, your "I could do this every day." You had the vision, the road map, the strategy. Then something called "life" happened: perhaps someone close to you got sick or passed away. Perhaps you had a big break up. Perhaps you didn't pass that exam the first time, or even the second.

When I was around four (according to my mother), I began declaring that I wanted to be a doctor. No one could convince me otherwise. However, the journey to this goal had a crazy route that my mind was unprepared for.

I was always smart. I graduated third in my high school class and finished Spelman College with above-average grades. But I couldn't seem to master the MCAT to save my life. I was told that, statistically, I would never become a doctor based on my test scores. I smiled, thanked them (whoever they were), and continued to press towards my goal. Because nothing ignites the go-getter's fuel as much as someone saying, "No, you can't."

By the grace of God, I got into medical school, but not in a way I expected or really wanted. I got into a school in Kansas City, thanks to Dr. Earnest Okeke who thought of me when he heard about a new Alabama pipeline for medical students. I had my doubts, but instead of holding onto my initial demands, this country girl let go of her own plans and said, "Okay, God, I trust You. I'm going to Kansas City."

To reach your maximum potential, you must make sacrifices. I'm sure you're already well familiarized with this. You've missed parties, family reunions, and vacations because you had that big goal in mind. Like me, you didn't stop until you proved all the naysayers and haters wrong. You became that doctor, that lawyer, that CEO, or that partner because you refused to give up. You go, girl.

It's this drive that keeps us going hard in our jobs. This feeling keeps us on the "Top 40 Under 40" list and always at the top of our profession. However, it only works and works well when we adjust the grip of our hands and allow God to execute His plan. I'm so thankful things didn't go "my way." I know sacrifice and struggle, so I have a deeper appreciation for favor, blessings, and unapologetic success, all of which I've thankfully been given a lot!

Think About It

[1] Have you given up on reaching your goals? What goals have you kept putting on the back burner because something else came up?

[2] What can you do to meet and exceed these goals, personally and professionally? List any classes or educational advances that would better your career and life.

Art of Delegation

As a working wife, you know that you must delegate work at your job and in your home if you have any chance of survival. If you choose not to, something goes lacking. Let's say it again: you can't do everything at 100% all the time! There will eventually be no more of you to give. To live healthier and happier lives, let's admit that asking for help is sometimes necessary and is in no way a sign of weakness.

I remember the first time my husband hired someone to clean our house. I kept it clean somewhat, but he was talking about a deep clean. I was so hurt, so upset, so "I can't believe him." Until I came home one day and the walls looked whiter, the stove was cleaned out, places were dusted that I couldn't even reach. My husband said to me, "You work way too hard. Getting someone to help us in this area frees you up some."

Just like that, a light bulb came on. Whether it was freeing me up to work harder or to have more time with him (this was pre-child), that extra help added days onto my overall life. Two weeks later, I asked the woman who'd made our house new to come back and, just like that, I had help again. I didn't feel guilty for needing it and I appreciated her because she was taking care of one thing on my to-do list. And you know how we are about marking off that to-do list. That was major for me!

There are many services that take care of a lot of "smaller" needs that are crucial to maintaining the flow of your household. There are grocery delivery services that you pay a little extra for, but prevent you from spending half your night in the store. There are home meal delivery services that have recipes and ingredients delivered to your door, so you're ready to start cooking whenever you're free. Remember, you're paying for convenience. Don't worry about what others say and do what's best for you to make your home flow smoother. My mom says that the grocery delivery service just makes us lazier, but I say, "No, ma'am!" It makes me smarter and no one has to pay for it but us. She now agrees and understands since she's already a Master Working Wife.

Make adjustments to ensure your peace of mind. Don't compare yourself to other wives, working or not. Try asking for help and watch yourself be set free little by little. And freedom usually isn't free at all. It comes with a price.

Think About It

[1] What can you delegate? Make a list and start Googling the pros and cons of each service.

[2] Getting more help will allow you to have more time to do *what* for yourself?

Raising a Brilliant Kid

Whether you've waited to have kids or you've always wanted them, we all have one thing in common: we want brilliant kids. Until someone can prove otherwise, our kids are brilliant to us just by saying, "Mama." But the actuality of raising a "brilliant" kid is easier prayed for than obtained. We all have great goals of raising doctors, lawyers, or accountants but then they reach their terrible twos or threes and you wonder, "What did I do to deserve this?" We still love them so much and so hard that no one better ever try and tell us they are not brilliant. Maybe bad and brilliant but they are definitely brilliant!

There is no manual, no guide, no reader's blueprint on how to raise kids. We are left with our own step-by-step trial and error system to try and figure out how to get it right. In order to have brilliant kids, we must often sacrifice time, money, and energy to make sure they are in the best schools, are active in extracurriculars, and have the best tutors (we need tutors at a young age nowadays). With these costs, we must work more to give our kids opportunities that we might have not had in our own childhoods and spend less time with them. So, we miss a few recitals or ball games, and where do we find ourselves? Drowning in that dreadful Mommy guilt.

So, what do you do to raise a brilliant child while being a happy working wife? First of all, give your child the benefit of the doubt: he or she will likely adjust to your frequent absence, so don't become overwhelmed with guilt. Second, think about what you're doing to help them adjust. Are you just handing them tablets and phones to entertain them for hours at a time? Research shows that too much screen time can be bad for children's overall mental health; besides, in the advent of smart boards at school, kids are already getting a substantial amount of screen time before they even get home.

In our house, we do not let our daughter watch more than one thirty-minute television show after she gets home from school. And if she chooses to watch one show, she can't play with the iPad. We do this because we found that, the more television she watched at home, the more issues she had in school. Limiting her screen time has helped her ability to focus and allows her to not be so overly stimulated. We also invest in more paperback books for her rather than just allowing her to read books on Kindles and other tablets. You can see that we must find a fine balance between too much and just right; if the scales are off, the consequences can be detrimental to our little brilliant babies.

Third, and once again, *never compare!* Comparison will kill any expectations, for yourself and for your child. There are many strong-willed kids out there who are brilliant in their own right, but have a lot of issues containing themselves. I could write a whole different book about how strong-willed my kid is. She teaches us so much but keeps us on our toes and has shown us that there is so much more to child rearing than statements like "Because I said so." Rearing techniques that were used on my husband and me when we were younger don't work. What worked for the kid next door doesn't necessarily work. And it doesn't have to! Like I said there is no manual whatsoever. As you decide rearing techniques, have a conversation with your husband to see what common ideals and expectations you share, and decide what's best for your particular family. Don't compare your parenting skills and don't compare you kids!

This should continue beyond toddlerhood into the pre-teens, teens, young adulthood, and so forth. Raising a brilliant kid and maintaining a happy marriage actually have a lot more in common than you think: it's about setting realistic and detailed expectations as a family and meeting unmet expectations together, one by one.

Think About It

[1] Have you discussed child-rearing tactics with your husband? If so, what plans have you made? If not, grab a glass of wine and start talking. List what you both consider acceptable practices. What are your negotiable and non-negotiable rules?

[2] What resources can you use to be better at time management? How can you free up time from work to meet your children's major events and milestones?

Bonus

TEN COMMANDMENTS OF THE WORKING WIFE

I. Thou shalt have affirmations daily.

II. Thou shalt make enough time for thyself.

III. Thou shalt make thy husband feel like he is a priority.

IV. Thou shalt always be honest with thyself.

V. Thou shalt never compare.

VI. Thou shalt commit to making sex a priority.

VII. Thou shalt schedule girls' time once a quarter (at least).

VIII. Thou shalt keep thyself fly (mind, body, and spirit).

IX. Thou shalt not work thyself to death.

X. Thou shalt be willing to ask for help when overwhelmed.

Thank You

Thank you, working wives, from the bottom of my heart for purchasing and reading this book. Thank you to my prayer warrior Michelle Johnson for covering this project. Thanks to my virtual assistant, Keundra Golden, for your help with this project. Huge thank you to my office manager, Maranda Pruitt, for keeping my head screwed on my head!

This is my first book, so I would love your feedback to continuing growing as an author (don't be scared! I can take it). Whether you liked my book or not, I hope you learned something new about the importance of balancing life as a working wife. It's an amazing job, isn't it? Continue thinking of these ideas and spread the word!

Dr. Kre is super busy! I'm either seeing a patient in my office, doing an online, print, radio, or TV media interview, or putting on my weekly Doctor Kre & Me show. However, I am expanding my reach by offering one-on-one coaching to other working wives and teaching a master class called the Wife Mindshift. Let's stay connected so I can keep you updated on my activities and fabulousness.

Here's how:

Website:	www.doctorkre.com
Facebook:	m.facebook.com/ Doctor Kre
Twitter:	@doctorkre
Instagram:	@doctorkre
Google+:	Doctorkre
LinkedIn:	Doctor Kre
Pinterest:	Doctor Kre
YouTube:	www.youtube.com/+doctorkre

About Doctor Kre

Dr. Ankrehah Trimble Johnson, aka Dr. Kre, is a Board-Certified Family Medicine Physician, public speaker, life coach, wife, and mother. In 2017, she earned the titles of *B-Metro* magazine's Top Doctors in Medicine and Top Women in Medicine, and Trademark Women of Distinction Honors for her dedication to answering questions about common medical conditions and bringing awareness to the importance of healthy lifestyles. She shares her medical expertise through her Facebook Live series, Dr. Kre & Me. She also mentors small groups of working wives to help them obtain balance and harmony between their work, home, and personal lives.

Dr. Ankrehah Trimble Johnson, DO

Dr. Johnson resides in Trussville, Alabama, with her husband and daughter. She earned her Doctor of Osteopathic Medicine degree from Kansas City University of Medicine and Biosciences and completed her residency at St. Vincent's East Hospital in Birmingham, Alabama. This is her first published work.

CREATING DISTINCTIVE BOOKS WITH INTENTIONAL RESULTS

We're a collaborative group of creative masterminds with a mission to produce high-quality books to position you for monumental success in the marketplace.

Our professional team of writers, editors, designers, and marketing strategists work closely together to ensure that every detail of your book is a clear representation of the message in your writing.

Want to know more?
Write to us at info@publishyourgift.com
or call (888) 949-6228

Discover great books, exclusive offers, and more at
www.PublishYourGift.com

Connect with us on social media

@publishyourgift

www.ingramcontent.com/pod-product-compliance
Lightning Source LLC
Chambersburg PA
CBHW071541080526
44588CB00011B/1751